L'heure Bleue
The Blue Hour

∞

The Collected Poems
Of Roland Verfaillie

Vol.3

Copyright © 2011 Purple Onion Press
All rights reserved

Published by Purple Onion Press

San Francisco, CA

Toronto, Canada

Designed and produced by Sigmund Rich, Purple Onion Press

Other works by Roland Verfaillie published by Purple Onion Press:

The Lie (screenplay)

The book of job(s)

The second book of job(s)

Hill of Sorrow/Mountain of Joy (Collected Poems)

Waking Up In Dreams (Collected Poems)

No part of this book may be reproduced, stored in any retrieval system, or transmitted in any form, by any means, including mechanical, electronic, recording, or otherwise, without written permission of the publisher.

Writers Guild of America, East, Inc.

Registration Number: 135850

Date Registered, November 18, 2011

L'heure Blue/The Blue Hour
ISBN 978-0-9787085-5-9

Contents	Page
Introduction	5-6

Our Autumn Season:

Song of the Late Harvest	9-17
Swift is Time	18-24
Attraction to the Storm	25-30
Lone Wolf	31-35
Greatly Insignificant	36-42
Lost Generation	43-49
Death Star	50-57
Racing the Clouds	58-60
Walking at Dusk	61-66
Acid Winds	67-69

Winter Discontent:

Blind Intent	71-72
Waiting for…	73-76
Related to Sacred Places We have Traveled	77-87
Speak False, Love True	88-92
Judas Kiss	93-98
Haiku…Yuck!	99

At sunrise everything is luminous but not clear. It is those we live with and love and should know who elude us. You can love completely without complete understanding. – A River Runs Through it"
» Norman Maclean

L'heure Bleue

The Blue Hour

The L'heure Bleue is the term that painters and photographers use to refer to twilight. The period of the day, between dawn and sunrise, and sunset and dusk, when the quality of ambient light creates artwork in the sky, and confirms the beauty of the world. It isn't so much a number by which to set the clock – mere reference points by which to mark the start and end of the day - as it is a state of mind. To the geophysicist, twilight is the geometric center of the sun relative to the mathematical horizon. There are computations based on degrees, angles and latitudes which determine the brightness and dullness of the light on the horizon. There are stratospheric aerosols and dust which influence the pallet of colors available to nature's artist. It is as if a dimmer switch is slowly turned; beginning bright with civil twilight, moving to midpoint at nautical twilight, and ending with darkest phase at astronomical dust. It is during the civil twilight that the brightest stars appear. When Venus glitters like a diamond, when we gaze upon the "morning star," turn on our porch lights and greet our neighbors with, "good evening."

I chose, "L'heure Bleue," as the title for Volume 3 of my poems because the poems seemed to echo with the resonance associated with the twilight hours. The Blue Hour conjures feelings of calm, tranquility and contemplation. Simultaneously there is a melancholy undertone that I associate with 'blues' music, the dobro guitar and a hound dog sleeping on the porch. Perhaps during this time of the day it just takes too much energy to be enthusiastic about anything. This quiet time of mind often invites rumination as we begin and end each day. When one is likely to interrupt the trance of tranquil meditation and take a busy inventory which calls forth the day's lessons in humility and more than a few regrets. I don't get morose and overly self –conscious when waking to the sunrise or while watching the sunset from the creaking glider on my veranda. Like I said, I associate freely during the twilight time, I don't analyze. And I don't over-think and expatiate like I'm doing now. I would like the twilight to be that which gives resonance to beauty and art for its own sake; not crowd it with personal significance, or invade it with the day's agenda. I want to break the habit of inventing constant distractions. But we can no longer leave the world alone and not infect it with interpretation, than we can control the setting and rising of the sun and the moon. Even these beautiful interstices that are like pauses between two notes of music become subjected to our habitual need to define what is fundamentally ineffable. Can I describe my favorite sunset? Which one? My favorite that is purple and black with strokes of tangerine applied with St. Berward's inspired brush, and captured on a photograph or artist's canvas?

The dawn and the dusk are immutable and always escape capture… Like sunlight through a prism or oil floating on the meniscus of a rain puddle. It is one of our rare, ephemeral and transitory experiences; not localized in place and time. The twilight is synonymous with the pause between heartbeats and the proverbial calm before the storm. However brief these respites may be, it is upon them we so depend for all the rest which follows. No one can predict for certain, that he will see another sunrise after the dusk. We hope for the chance that we will. We can say with impunity that the sun will rise tomorrow with or without us. It is about the impermanence of our lives, and its acceptance that I write. It is a challenge to our denial that we will end one day as surely as the sun will set, and that the beauty of the world will continue on without us. It is between pillar and post – sunrise and sunset - we go, each day until we're laid to rest. This is what I write about.

Our Autumn Season

My sorrow, when she's here with me,
Thinks these dark days of autumn rain
Are beautiful as days can be;
She loves the bare, the withered tree;
She walks the sodden pasture lane.

Robert Frost
My November Guest.

Song of the Late Harvest

Together we prepare the fruits,
Of the harvest,
Ripened through the longanimity,
Of a fickle season,
With the stained skin,
Of their imperfect flesh,
All freckled and mottled,
Nicked and furrowed,
Many, pecked by birds,
Drilled by insects,
Blemished by the others,
Who've taken the first bite.

I sing the lyrics,
Of an old-time harvest ritual,
Humming a tune,
When the words are forgotten,
And she takes this for a dirge,
Because she says,
I sound,
 Like a wailing mourner,
At a Corsican wake.

She takes her cue,
Too easily,
To bring in a chorus of her own,
And seats them at the paring bench,
To join her in a sad and dark refrain,

Her music… she conducts,
With a sickle and a scythe,
More like the reaper of death,
Than of fruits, gourds,
And grain,
It is my love's attitude,
That they're one,
And the same.

She spills the nectar,
Red as blood,
From rendered flesh,
Of blistered fruit,
Beneath dark skin,
That she has peeled,
With a finger knife,
Sharp as the talon,
Of a red tail hawk,
And gored with a blade,
Of cold steel.

I asked her for warm linden tea,
And bread baked fresh,
From the oven,
But instead,
She brought me bitter wormwood,
And a bajan cake,
Made out of roasted corn,
Sunflower seeds,
And ergot of rye.

After a brutal assault,
On the grove and the field,
Our bench is a haven,
Beneath the shade,
Of the chestnut tree.

Left in the shed are the weapons:
The scythe; and the shear;
The Bushmaster,
And Mohawk machetes.

We are too small for the columbine,
Better is the gentle hand,
That picks the apple, peach,
And the pear,
Too rough is the truck,
With the Chevy horse-powered shaker,
And hydraulic cherry picker.

My love berates me,
For pining the loss,
Of my stone knife,
Long pole, and axe,
And for the stupidly,
Of considering,
The metate and mano,
When commercial grinders,
And sifters,
Are more thorough,
And much faster.

She, like Eris, brings strife,
To me,
And like Geras,
She hastens the aging,
Of the harvest fruit,
And corrupts it prematurely,
On the vine.
She could be the daughter,
Of Nemesis,
Born of a baneful night,
Causing darkness at noon,
And heartache at night,
To Semele the seed sower,
And me.

I would rather see,
The fields of grain,
Waving in the wind,
On a late summer day,
Preamble to the death,
Of Ceres,
And the lament of Demeter,
No less willing,
To send the cutter,
With the scythe,
To do the deed,
Though fully present,
Gaze fixed upon,
A golden carpet,
Rolled out upon,
A fertile prairie.

Now the fields,
Are laid fallow,
And the orchard branches bare,
Decimated by the hungry man,
The infestation of the locust,
And the oily,
Smoking ravages,
Of voracious farm machines.

The fruits left behind,
On the vine,
On the tree,
Or in the field,
We do not see,
But catch on the currents,
In the scent that travels,
To our senses,
Treacle sweet,
Pleasant…at first,
And then, like a rotting corpse,
Left to decay,
In open charnel houses,
It wrenches in my gut,
Like a snake lying coiled,
For the strike.

The fruit it lies there,
Unfit for the living to consume,
But for the vermin to devour.
Like road kill,
Or the accidental murder,
Of the rabbit, the field mouse,
Or the garden snake,
Cut down,
By the cabbage knife,
In the busy hands,
Of cutters,
Rushing through the fields,
To bring the late crop in.

Cloying is the nectar,
Of the dying fruit,
Left to rot,
A smell like never,
That has ever assailed,
Your delicate senses,
Unless you are descended,
From the undertaker,
That once embalmed the pharaohs;
Stuffing them,
With nacron, leaves and honey…
Exquisite cadavers…
Exuding the sweet redolence,
Of precious myrrh,
And frankincense.

Fruit once beautiful,
Refulgent with life...

Redolent as the blossom,
Perfumed as the attars...

Swing like censers,
In the breeze...

That by-and by...

Weigh more heavily,
On the branch.

The fruits of the fallen,
And the dying,
Drop like suicide jumpers,
From the trees,
Or remain impaled,
Upon the bush,
To ferment in juices,
Cooked by the sun.

Heady nectars.
Bleed through cracked skin,
And seep through injured soil,
To nourish the exhausted ground,

Gaea,
Goddess of the fertile earth,
We pray,
Will be requited,
And grant us,
A plentiful harvest,
Again …
Next year.

Wormy flesh,
Fought over by the Keres,
(Death's daimons),
With such gnashing teeth,
And claws,
Their thirst not slaked,
For only blackened flesh,
But rather blood,
That is the fruity nectar.

Is this gloomy gothic fantasy?
Or just the bird,
And the raccoon,
Returning to obtain satiety,
To further fatten,
On the fallen and the ripened.

Easier to feast upon it,
On the ground,
As it is for the harvester,
To pare his fruit,
At the cutting bench,
Beneath the shaded,
Chestnut tree.

My love,
She thinks me morbid,
For these thoughts,
Shared at the harvest,
But these are not my own,
Original thoughts,
But those inspired by my love,
Who shares the paring bench,
Whose complaints,
About the harvest,
She thinks are mine,
When only I was humming,
To myself,
Some harvest tune,
The words to which,
I had forgotten.

Swift is Time

The direction of time for me,
Is straight ahead,
And is as swift,
As the flight of an arrow,
Sailing to the mark,
That is the heart,
Of some dark dream,
From which,
No one awakens.
A consubstantial corpse,
Crumbled to bone shard and ash,
Still cooling from the gas flames,
Of cremation,
Alive with heat,
If not with possibility,
For new life,
Or for penance,
Or redemption.

My death was born,
A branch,
Of slender ash
Protruding from a sapling,
Green and tender,
Nourished by the dew drops,
After April morning rain,

When the sun,
Is the yellow-orange color,
Of egg-yolk broken open,
On the jagged edge,
Of the faraway,
Shimmering…
Horizon.

There were green buds,
Like teenage acne,
Erupting from its skin,
From which leaves,
Soon appeared,
Pinnately delicate,
Like infants' fingers,
Tugging at the hem,
Of the meadow mist,
Which rose like a canvas sail,
To catch the morning breeze.

And soon,
A full-grown hand,
Reached out
To grasp migrating birds,
Its branches finally thick enough,
To cradle nests of sparrows.

Mighty became the ash,
In whose shadows crops,
Would die,
And ravens perched,
Atop the highest branches,
Would rejoice,
At killing all the sparrows.

Time is swift to you and me,
But not to the ash,
The lifetime of birds,
And the totality of creation.
Say, the ash is the World Tree,
Called Yggdrasil,
Its sap fermented is,
The Meade of Inspiration,
But the tree is not kind,
To an inattentive man,
Stopping beneath thick boughs,
Of this reputed Widow Maker.

My life did not end,
Beneath the ash's knarred branches,
While studying a leafy-lacework-tapestry,
As tarnished sunlight,
Cast mottled, dancing shadows,
On the ground.

Time is not swift,
Or slow,
Nor kind,
Or cruel,
Yet passes quick…
For me, now,
That novelty has turned to rust,
The chrome,
Of every dull, new day.

The ash gave up a stout bow,
To the hunter,
Who makes arrows,
For an atlatl,
Not the long bow.

Death prefers an atlatl,
Because it's silence,
Sends less warning,
To the victim,
Whose tell-tale heart,
Beneath his breastplate,
Is a target for the archer.

The pace of this slow arrow,
Is like a quartz clock ticking,
Ticking down the minutes,
To the hallowed,
 Midnight hour.

The sound of this slow arrow,
Sounds no shrill alarm,
Save for the quieting,
Of that beating heart,
Growing cold,
Beneath,
The rusted iron breastplate,
That's no barrier to the arrow.

Death is our intention,
Decried by nature's eyes,
Its execution our design;
Beginning with a birth,
That cries out,
Our first Confiteor,
The outrage insincere,
Mock pleasures,
Then conduced,
To make us want to live,
While wear and tear and time,
Coax us to the brink,
To rue the day,
And regret the fact,
That we were ever born.

You think this is a poem,
Of simple life and death,
Of classical trials,
And banal tribulations,
Where time, gravity,
And nature,
Conspire to end our days,
When truth be told,
We made it so,
Even accelerating time,
To hasten our demise.

Our model for creation,
Along with how to live,
Is constructed in a box,
Filled with bread and water,
Cars and clocks.

Our internal thinking,
Weakly rational,
Imposes upon the world,
Our flaws, our shallow vanities,
Our childish illusions,
Vain conceits,
Intentions, plans,
And actions.

The ash still stands,
Timeless and alone,
Unconscious but for us,
Who gave it everything:
Its family, genus,
And entire species.

We invented myths and rites,
For it,
And gave it Heartwood and a soul,
Found uses for its lumber,
Such as furniture,
For our homes.

We value its beauty,
Durability and strength,
Strong wood from which,
The hunter made the bow,
And fletched and hafted arrows.

The archer who draws the bow,
And sends the missile,
To the heart,
To becomes mans',
Hired assassin.

Attraction to the Storm

It was a murrey-colored sky turned black,
Before the heavens set to flame,
The raw and fibrillose heart,
That had barely beat or echoed,
Its dull vibration,
Within his heaving breast.

From the lightsome to pitch-black,
His energies did seek,
The eternal dark,
Into which the failing heart takes rest.

Until a vault of darkest night,
Drew shades upon the hour of the day,
And rent the fabric of sheer air,
And filled it up,
With dust and ice.

He is deafened,
By a cacophony of many shofars,
Sounding from a mountain peak,
Which neither sand nor rock,
Had piled there.

From where perhaps,
Zeus throws,
A lightning spear,
Aiming for the quiet shade,
That is a target,
By its shapelessness,
Its emptiness, vacuity,
And space.

More dangerous,
To the gods,
And to the man,
To aim the spear too high,
And chance to pierce the skin,
Of Heavens fury,
And excite this dull demesne,
With lightning, rain,
And thunder.

This is what he might attract,
Who is content with calmer weather,
Never taking risks for greater pleasure,
Satisfied with the company of angels,
And the Saints,
Eager to enlist,
And retire with the army,
Of the just.

His sky is like a looking glass,
Opaque with fug,
Obscuring the heavens,
Starry night with wet medallions,
Of lichen and rust,
Expelled by the breath,
Of fetid marshes, acid bogs,
And cemetery fog.

He breathes deeply,
The poisons of methane gas,
And succumbs to radon's,
Hidden presence,
In the rocks beneath his feet.

He thinks sweetly fragrant,
Is the charnel stench,
Of a man and a woman,
Lain early and exposed,
Within the catacomb,
Because he is deceived,
By the treacle sweet scent,
Of moldering flowers,
Arranged in cooper urns.

He knows what it will take,
To turn the screw,
And reverse the slow descent,
Of his slow death.
What power it will take,
That may lie beyond his grasp,
Or his ability to handle.

There are powers of attraction,
That may restore,
The still life of a man,
More likely than a bowl,
Of waxen fruit,
Or wilted flowers.

More power than it takes,
To raise fine hair,
Brushed with silk,
Or produce weak static,
Caused by stroking coarse wool,
With golden amber bars.
No fossil of a Cambrian wasp,
Has been resurrected,
From the resin of lost time,
To fly with grace,
Or sting with venom.
Not even for…
A fleeting moment.

Look man!
To the plains,
Beyond the steep rise.

See the lightning set fire,
To the prairie grasses,
Listen to the distant thunder,
Feel the supersonic wave,
That sends shockwaves through,
The world's thin mantel,
And restores the rhythm,
Of its regenerate heart.

Do not fear the upper regions,
Of the heavens,
When they speak,
And wake you from your sleep,
These are not fairytale dreams,
 Of sprites, and elves,
But blue jets,
Of superheated mass,
Which melt the pith,
Of angry clouds,
And light up a starless night.

These are the voltages,
Delivered by the plasma storms,
Of the sun,
And the atmosphere of Venus.
Enough to power,
The houses of Corinth,
Enough to ignite,
The incandescent sphere,
That is a soul,
Now Burning,
With Saint Elmo's fire.

He will be restored,
If he should chance the storm,
Unafraid to stand in the rain,
Fearless of the rise time,
When the lightning,
Nears the oak,
The elm and the pine,
Daring enough to live,
In the village of Kifuka,
In the heart of the Congo,
Where the lightning strikes…
Most often.

Lone Wolf

Wolf…you run alone,
You are a solitary one,
Unlike your brothers and sisters,
Who understand the needs of one,
Are satisfied by the many.

You run the Wolf Road of the Milky Way,
Above the game trails favored by the pack,
Your claws are like flints striking steel,
Showering sparks upon,
The bruised and blackened clouds.
Your howls shatter the stillness,
Like the deafening clap,
Of a giant's hand cuffing the ear,
Of a mischievous child.

You, Wolf,
Sunder the eerie silence,
Of the woods and plains,
And rear on haunches,
That extends your,
Height and reach,
From level ground,
To mountain peaks.

You wolf,
Who to the child lying in the grass,
Is a malevolent transformation,
Rising from dark instincts
In a thunder head
Resembling the Fenrir,
Of Norse legend.

Wolf, you are strong,
Yet vulnerable
And in peril…
Chased by Odin's son,
Who aims a dagger at your heart,
And seeks to rip your jaws apart,
So you will not howl into the darkness,
Mistaking you,
For whatever else it is,
That average men and women fear.

Vanquishing easily the loner,
Who's broken rank,
With the pack,
And will not keep their company,
Or bay in concert,
With his brothers and his sisters.

Pack, I run from you,
I do not chase the setting sun,
I do not run the Milky Way
And stand up tall on haunches,
To raise myself above the rest.

Pack, I run against the wind,
For it is safer when hunted,
In the winter,
For what warmth,
Our guards and undercoats provide,
To the heartless, cold, and ruthless.

Pack, I leave you far behind,
To chase what lies beyond,
The crimson curtain,
Of our prairie,
Now bathed in flames,
As dead, dry grasses burn.

Pack, I choose to use our gifts,
And hunt the regal beasts,
That prowl the woods and plains,
I long to taste the blood of caribou,
And slay the bison, elk, and beaver.

You pack, who are content,
To dine upon,
The muskrat, mouse and vole.

My finer gifts,
I would bestow,
Upon the families of the hunter,
To search the mudslide and the avalanche,
To retrieve their dead and dying,
But I will not serve the hunter,
And his family.
Who would rather wipe their muddy boots,
On my skinned hide,
And lie down on me,
While stretched out resting,
By the hearth.

My snout pointed in the wind,
Is served a ripe and redolent banquet,
That if I keep my course tonight,
Will feed me in the morning.
I told you I prefer the taste,
Of fresh killed flesh,
Not carrion,
Crawling with worms and maggots.

Pack, I run from you,
Whose mother is the bitch,
Who ate her pups,
When there was drought and famine.
Pack, our mother is,
Mai-cob the witch,
In familiar wolf's clothing,
Not the loving Lupa,
Of ancient Roman myth.
She will sink her canine teeth,
Into the scruff of her young pups,
And carry them to the river,
And drown them in the currents.

Pack, I escaped this fate,
By the grace of Tiberinus,
Who led me through the streams,
And down the westerly flowing rivers,
And I listened to the wind,
Telling me to run,
And so I set my sight,
Upon a mottled copper sunset,
That guttered like a thousand votive candles,
Placed upon an altar.

Greatly Insignificant

I was born into the world,
Valued by my progenitors,
Destined for success,
Graduated with honors,
Given rank and status,
Licensed, and insured,
Serialized by random numbers,
Which quantify my life,
And offers proof,
Of my existence.

I am counted in the census,
Am a registered voter,
Have bank accounts,
And credit cards,
And a social security number.

I am energetic and dynamic,
Going places,
Running,
Only briefly resting
Drafting in the slip stream,
Of measured time.

Tractable on a GPS,
You can locate my position,
In degrees, hours,
Minutes, and seconds,
Cornering me,
In the confined spaces,
Of this oh so infinite,
And expansive universe.

Where…
From the supernal,
Vantage point,
Beyond the event horizon,
I do not measure greater,
Than half the width of a photon,
Less than a neutrino,
Smaller than an electron,
Imperceptible as a quark.

I am not even a mite,
Or a splinter of cold flint,
Even less…
The phantom,
Quantum string,
That dances like a floater,
In the aqueous humor,
In the eye of God.

I dare not,
Cast a glance,
Upon the welkin,
To count the stars,
Or name the constellations.

The Hubble,
Wouldn't notice me,
If I were clutched in Orion's
Mighty outstretched hand,
Or seated in the lap,
Of distant Virgo.

I crouch beneath,
A sphere of solar wind,
That sears my scalp,
And causes me,
To gasp for air,
When Kuiper's belt,
Is tightened.

Lo and behold…
The eye of God,
Through which I see,
The significance of me,
Is when assayed,
By the atom smasher.

For I am a universe,
Unto myself,
Composed of many molecules,
Reducible to atoms,
Made of quarks,
Shrunk to electrons,
Parsed as protons,
And compacted,
Into neutrons.

What am I if,
I can't be seen,
Serially numbered,
Or addressed,
And beyond the realm,
Of measure?

Where no device,
Can locate,
The important,
Non-substantial me…
Because it hasn't,
Been discovered,
And lies not here,
Nor far beyond,
The vault of Heaven.

I can conceive,
Me standing,
In a fun house,
Full of mirrors,
Which multiply,
My dimensions,
And fragment,
The basic elements,
Of which I'm made,
Ad infinitem.

Where the fabric,
Of my make-up,
Is disassembled,
And the invention,
Of my identity,
Dissolves into,
A Particle of Creation.

I might could become,
Through further,
Countless,
Mass reductions,
And Sub-atomic,
Permutations,
The transitory,
Elusive boson,
Theorized by Higgs.

Soon I will push,
Against the wall,
Of another universe,
Casting a dark spot,
Like a shadow,
On an X-ray,
That warns me,
That some malignant,
Replicating tumor,
Could metastasize…

End my world,
Darken the sun,
And thrust me,
Into the void,
That is the birth canal,
The worm hole,
Or the Mother,
Through which,
Another universe is born,
And of which I am,
It's beating solar heart,
When on the other side.

From where…

Again…

On infant hands and knees,
I peer,
Into the starlit heavens,
Vast and elegant,
And begin to estimate,
The size of it,
And question,
The significance,
Of *Me*.

Lost Generations

I live among a generation,
Lost to a cause,
I never did believe in,
And never thought was just,
And should have listened,
To an old soldier's wisdom,
Before I joined.

I was convinced that enlisting,
Putting on the uniform,
And bearing arms,
Would complete me as a man.

Appealing isn't it?
When flush and spry at eighteen,
Years of age,
Fusible as brass,
Poured into a bullet mould.

Rushing like blood to the cock,
Is the clarion call to war,
As the heart beat quickens to the cadence,
Of the fife and drum,
Depicted by the smiling wounded,
In the Norman Rockwell print.

I am happy *now* to find myself,
Among the few others of my kind,
Who sit with wine,
At polished tables,
In cafes,
By the tarns of the Rhine,
Or quaff a pint of Guinness,
In the pubs along the hythes,
Of the Avon.

I am far from the radix of the warrior,
That was first the womb,
And then the Conexes,
Pitched like the tents,
Of Union soldiers,
In the backyards,
Of Confederate neighbors.

I am no longer thrilled by the tempests of war,
Or excited by fire,
No longer intrigued by the shapes,
Assumed by the cordite fog,
Drifting across the desert,
Like horsemen of the Khan.

I anchored against sandstorms,
And braced myself against the onslaught,
Of the locusts.
I shook out my bedroll,
And still do,
To chase away the spider and the viper,
The way the towel heads did to me.

Never was I chastened,
By the evangelism of nation building,
Reluctant to embrace the crackpot scheming,
Of the politicians.

Who's eager to be expelled,
As afterbirth,
Of new democracies,
Born with the temperament,
Of crack babies,
Destined for delinquency.

The acclivity of my politics,
Like my evolution,
Is a burrow in the valley,
Of the ocean's Marianna Trench.

I aspire to no great height,
And choose to stay below,
The threshold of notice,

Not a visible target,
Seen perched upon the aiguilles,
The spire, the campanile,
Or the tower.

As primal man,
I defy exact description,
Though prefer a photograph of me,
When I was twenty-one,
To illustrate the point.
Then flush and spry,
Fresh with the gene,
Called SRY,
That produced the virile form,
Defeminized in the factory,
Of my mother's womb.
Born with surety and purpose,
To be more aggressive, self-assured,
And more arrogant than the gentler,
Other gender,

That plays second string,
To epics, English tales,
The Bhagavad Gita,
Mohammed's teachings,
And the Hagakure.

What has happened to me,
That I have become a symbol,
Called a hero,
For nothing close to valor,
A shadow figure,
Imposed upon a mythic warrior tale.
And discontentedly so.

For hailed are the conquests,
Forgotten are the losses,
Though unerringly remembered,
In the poems, the ballads,
And in the books,
That have been written,
Glorifying war,
Knowing what harm may come,
To innocent children,
Who buy the fiction,
Or foolishly aspire,
To be the hero,
Of such tales.

"Beware," I tell them,
"Do not follow the smoky traces,
Of fires;" their burned out ashes,
Recently extinguished,
Atop a blackened ridge,
For fire has been known,
To spontaneously re-ignite,
And blossom into flame,
Burning the curious,
Who come too near.

Rather they would early on,
Find a café table,
Under an umbrella by the Sarne,
And ply the arts,
Of juggling, street music,
And magic,
Along the rues,
And boulevards.

Let them spread,
Joy and mystifying acts,
Of diplomacy through kindness,
Not democracies, new nations,
Or Gideon bibles.

Keep journals,
Of your travels,
Write with sharpened graphite pencils,
Not breeches greased with oil,
Locked and loaded with ammunition.
How ruthless is the combat tourist,
Who invades the town,
And breaks down doors,
When a good map,
A stout walking stick,
And a gentle knock upon the door,
Will do.

DIY Death Star   **Level**: Easy   **Cost**: Everything   **Materials**: Hindu Trinity; earthmover; Round-Up; Monsanto seed stock
Time to Complete: 200 years (almost finished).

Death Star

A death's head,
Leans in seductively,
To kiss the earth,
With lips of gothic black,
Like oiled lipstick,
Smeared across,
M'Nai Shiva's mouth,
Applied by a sloppy hand,
Not by god,
That made a perfect universe,
Who, if the make-up artist,
Would have made the lips,
Voluptuous,
Roseate as sunset,
Warmed by the near-by sun,
Moistened from a ladle,
Of spring rain,
Raised from a world,
Whose mild seasons,
Would give lips and life,
A more delicate beauty.

It was not the steady hand of god,
But the clumsy fist of man,
Who put a gothic face upon creation,
Using tools beginning with stone axes,
Later picks and shovels,
Now machines,
That can displace 400 tons,
Of earth, and rocks, and trees,
In a minute.

Glory Be! to the gods,
Of the new creation,
With names like,
Bharat, LTD., and Krupp,
Progenitors of India's gods,
And the numbered,
Great World Wars,
Whose Instruments,
Are employed,
In the deeds,
Of selfish men.
Relished by Siva,
While Lord Brahma,
And Lord Vishnu,
Watch idly amused.

It is not a warming globe,
But man's fire brand,
With which he signs his name,
And sears his initials,
In the earth's frail hide,
And standing back,
He marvels over his achievements,
One less stand of pines,
Another parking lot.

He is a man of prayer,
When praying for relief,
Against the draught,
His prayers answered,
By clouds of poison rain,
Bringing acid spears,
To pain the tender green.

He will not slash burn,
Without a purpose,
But to purify the land,
With ritual camphor oil,
Burning hotly,
Leaving no ash,
And no trace of the match,

And in the sacred conflagration,
Rid the pests:
The sunning snake,
The ground jay,
And the spotted owl.

Why devise yet,
Another senseless religion,
Made up of zealots who preach:
"Let us save every species,
From extinction!
Rather we should kill,
The devout,
And burn the liberals,
At the stake.

It is an unwise man,
Who defaces Dattatreya,
Believing that two faces,
Like two heads,
Are better than one,
And three is too many,
For a simple mind to grasp.
Disfigure Lord Vishnu,
And blind him,
To the acts of wonton ruin.

Recovery is divine,
So leave it to Lord Brahma,
To heal the sick,
And cure the blind.

Bless them all,
The good and the bad,
And let the evil men,
Atone upon their deathbeds,
And be granted absolution.

Clever is the man,
Who is agnostic,
Until the end's at hand.
Wiser is the mugwump.

Watch Lord Shiva,
Dance the jig,
And lead Dattatreya's dogs,
To hell,
To keep company,
With Lord Brahma,
For there he is imprisoned,
For the discriminate use of reason,
And the habit of creation,
Punished for interfering,
With our fundamental search,
For a blissful state of nothing.

It is not the garden pests,
Who spoil the crop.
Poor aphid, snail,
And caterpillar,
They take the rap.
Blame it on the small,
Conceal the mighty's work,
And grant Monsanto,
Exclusive patents,
Hefty profits,
And corporate tax cuts,
For producing pretty produce,
And a strain of yellow corn,
That is lethal,
To the worm,
Who dines on its ripe kernels.

Sorry will be the pre-school child,
Who bites,
His corn-fed friend.

Ah, who cares?
We are just part-time tenants,
Renting here.
Temporary occupants,
Of this fading blue-dot planet,
Shuttled here,
Before remembered time,

By green aliens;
No doubt,
Slum lords,
From some back-water galaxy,
Like Sagittarius.

We are the guest,
Who wears his muddy boots,
Into the house,
And props his feet,
Upon the coffee table,
Who wipes his mouth,
Across his filthy sleeve,
And blows his nose into his hand,
Before shaking yours,
And leaving,
After all your food,
And drink is gone.

We are destined for the heavens,
Where we'll rejoice,
With repented Hell's Angels,
Join the Tea Party choir,
Joyful in zero-gravity,
In the quivering red jelly,
Of our cosmic subtle bodies.

To hell with green earth,
Blue skies and clear waters,
For Mankind will embrace,
In the communal dance,
Of the blithe –zero--calorie,
And asexual,
Everlasting spirit.

This is man's curse,
Not his blessing.
Meaningless and empty,
Is the reward,
He cannot have,
Until he dies,
For I'd much rather dance,
In fields,
Of non-GMO grain,
With a flesh- and-blood woman,
Under blue skies and sunshine.

One up for a stroll,
On a path,
Through the woods,
Skipping with me,
With a song in our hearts.

Amen!

Racing the Clouds

My blood rushes,
Like a white-water river,
When chasing after clouds,
A foot-race never won.
Too impetuous,
Is the tempest.
Too competitive,
The Nephelai -
Too proud,
To allow a boy,
Like me,
To win.

Though...
I am not easy to discourage,
For I am:
A brawling;
Roaring;
Dancing boy,
On fire,
Daring thunderheads,
Swollen with rain,
To burst,
And douse the flames,
Licking furiously,
At my heels.

I am a brawling,
Irish kid,
Not sulky,
And full of tragedy,
And brooding,
Like the others,
Not a mewling,
Sucking at the tit,
Of me 'mum.
Now sneaking shots,
Of whiskey,
Distilled from sodden,
Ricks of rye,
Cooked to mash,
In me 'granddad's,
Copper still.

I am a drunken child,
Intoxicated,
With the thrill,
Of chasing after clouds,
Believing I will,
Win the race,
Though I pull a wagon,
Full of broken toys,
Which slows me down.

But...
I am a burning boy,
Dancing,
Spinning,
And running barefoot,
In a race,
Against,
Such clouds,
Which shape shift,
Into teddy bears,
And cuddly puppies,
In the imagination,
Of the peaceful child,
Lying in the grass,
Becoming arctic bears,
And fire-breath'n dragons,
To the brawling, sassy child,
Who chases after clouds.

Walking at Dusk

I stroll these streets at dusk,
Passing houses that conform,
To the boring plan,
Of some unimaginative architect,
Unattractive in the gloaming,
Of a dying day,
Under a moon,
The hue,
Of tarnished pewter,
Whose sickly glow,
Casts weak shadows,
On frost hove sidewalks.

Moon beams shimmer,
Through a silhouette of leaves,
Which seem to come alive,
And crawl along the ground,
Like swarms of,
 Japanese Beetles,
Chasing after scraps of dung,
Dropped from sleeping birds,
Perched in the branches.

I give wide berth,
To head-high hedges,
Arranged like prickly tare
To hide the pale,
And weathered siding,
Of some houses,
That were flooded in the spring,
And are not pretty,
To look at,
Even in the cosmetic forgiveness,
Of the muted,
Light of the moon.

I am stalking the night,
Like some beleaguered spirit,
Freshly dug from the grave,
Fearful of the blinding sun,
Of a cloudless day,
And the hurry-up pace,
Of the living…
Afraid of becoming unemployed.

I am a peripatetic soul,
Unleashed from the wheel,
Of a servile job,
That will eventually,
Grind me down,

Allowing me to briefly rest,
Until the next,
Day's labor,
Makes the thwaite I clear,
Become a grave.

I walk in the solemn eve's embrace,
Romanced by violet, paper lanterns,
Draped beneath a roof,
Glowing eerily within,
Seemingly alive,
With the guttering flames,
Of tea candles
Though they are just,
Forgotten Christmas lights,
Damaged by the rains.

I stop briefly by a house,
From another age,
Once bathed,
In lambent candle light,
With an atmosphere suffused,
With the sulphuric scent,
Of curling sooty flames,
Of antique oil lamps.

I peer within,
As curtains part,
In the evening's balmy breeze,
And like the raven's head,
Tucked beneath its wing,
In sleep,
I am vigilant,
And catch a fleeting glimpse,
Of life within,
That I imagine,
Is trapped inside,
Like thrackscat ore,
Left behind,
In abandoned mines.

I surmise as I walk by,
This haunted dwelling,
That there are,
Echoes of Human hearts,
And speech,
Still lingering here,
Emitting heat,
From yesterday's fire,
That burned in the hearth,
And that I reconstruct,
In my imagination,

Like an infrared sensor,
Catching ghostly images,
Reliving their regrets.

I look closer,
And pretend,
I see a figure,
Looking like Osama Bin Laden,
In a bulls-eye,
Circumscribed upon an open doorway,
A curtain or a caftan,
Blown away in the crossfire,
By intruders bearing weapons,
Brought in from the streets,
The same I walk tonight.

A pool of ink,
Spreads across the balcony,
Following its imperfections,
Like a lazy stream,
That gathers in the hollow patch,
Of a hardened concrete slab,
And comes to rest.

It is the color red,
When in the light,
Viscous and sticky,
The spilt blood,
Of a controversial saint,
Depicted as a Moslem Satan,
But looking like Jesus Christ,
Before his crucifixion.

These are the tortured images,
Emerging from the shadows,
During an evening walk at dusk...

After watching to the 6 o'clock news.

Acid Winds

I run bare-foot over arid land,
Uneven, rough and rocky.
Parched like roasting paper,
Peeled from the bottom crust of bread,
Baked too long on the oven rack.
Like skipping across hot coals.

My skin is the caramelized color of smoke,
Cracked and crenulated,
Like burnt crust or shed skin,
Flaking and sloughing away to reveal,
The new flesh of a molting serpent,
Or the shucked gray earthly coil of a man,
Running through acid wind.

My soles seek purchase where there is no level ground.
I have not come upon a smooth worn path,
Not even faint game trails,
To show the way through the creosote bush,
The sage brush and forests of saguaro,
It is surely on the Devil's Highway that I run.

I feel the spines of the cactus,
Working their way through my tender arches
Like wood screws turning through bleeding sapwood.
Pain's cruel tender mercies,
Are numbness, shock and death,
Except for those who run long distances,
Through storms of acid wind.

Resistance diminishes the man, who runs head-long,
Against prevailing winds,
In opposition to the contours of unevenness,
Bending like smoke against obstructions in a wind tunnel,
With clothing turned to shredded rags,
Like Arab draping on a mannequin.
This effigy of me,
Whose painted eyes, and ruby lips,
Hide well the pallor mortis,
And preserve the desiccated corpse.

Acid wind is not kind to my complexion,
Causing fissures, open wounds and hands de-gloved,
Skinned alive by chemical taxidermy.
The long grey hair upon my head,
Trails like filaments of cotton thread,
Unwinding from a bobbin...
As I run faster through the acid wind.

My body's stain will be upon the wind,
Not silhouetted on the sand or on the canyon floor,
I will un-jacket sinew, fat and flesh,
And slash resistance in the deal,
Better to run against a raging acid wind,
And debride the wound by nature's quickest method,
Rather than be feast upon by vultures,
Wolves and worms,
And keep beyond the wiggle and the reach,
Of voracious coffin flies.

My bones bleach white as I run far,
My spirit close at hand,
The blazing sun will soon reduce,
My marrow into sand.
I then expect that I'll be free,
And cross the finish line,
Where east and west,
And north and south…,
Become a single point;
Where the wind grows still,
And light and darkness cease.

**falling leaves
hide the path
 so quietly
John Bailey**
Autumn, A Haiku Year.

Blind Intent

I meant to drive the wedge,
Into the pillar,
Causing it to rive,
And begin to crumble,
Hastening the time it took,
To lace it with the cracks and nicks,
Of hard wear,
Caused by disabuse.

I meant to weave,
That brace of thorns,
Around my lover's pillow,
Upon whose pretty face,
Deep cuts were scored,
By nature's brambles,
(That I did not create!),
To mark the deed.

I cultivated tender sprays,
Of wild blackberry,
Primrose,
And passionflower,
To protrude,
Through a copse,
Of sumac,
That I did not consider,
Cutting back.

And I watched it strangle,
The tender sprays I planted,
Only to grow thick,
By sun and rain,
And kill the best,
I grew,
Through my,
Neglect.

Waiting for…

While the woman waits,
She is spoiling the grandchildren,
While she sleeps,
She dreams an Argentine tango partner,
Or of meeting a former lover.

When she wakes,
She waits,
And while waiting,
She works a part-time job,
Applying poultices of mud,
Drawing creams and analgesic tonics,
To sooth the knotted sinew,
Of those wound too tight,
Or bound too early,
By the winding cloth.

While she waits,
She works,
Delivering the stillborn,
Trapped in voluntary lassitude,
Ensnaring both in the coils of concertina wire,
That sets fire to her joints,
And nicks the tender flesh,
Of healing hands,
 Massaging thorns and razors.

The woman waits,
Not to spoil the grandchildren,
Nor to sleep,
And dream a former lover,
Or wake to work on and on,
In endless days of caring after others,
Rarely collecting the collateral,
Of strangers that cannot break the habit of inertia,
For while she waits,
They rest assured,
That her devotion to their care,
Will bring her back to them again,
And she will greet them with false cheer,
And like them,
Become one too,
Who waits,
And works,
And gives no motion,
To an action more serene.

The man,
He doesn't wait,
Not there to spoil the grandchildren,
He sleeps beside a dream,
That shares a king sized bed,
With the partner of the passé noble.

When he wakes,
He works a full time job,
Shoveling hope to fill a valley of despair,
For those who will not lift a shovel,
Or build the bridge,
To transcend it on their own,
Unfamiliar with an excavator,
Other than the one,
That digs the grave.

He did not wait,
Although he misses the grandchildren,
And the woman who waits,
That dances in her dreams,
While imagining a fictive lover,
Working endless days,
Of caring after others,
That's not him.

So he waits for things to change,
And waits for work,
That is the same,
Still hauling buckets filled with the sludge,
Of the fetid and unwashed,
Belying the coxcomb languor he prefers,
Rather feinting the motion of spontaneous change,
 From the imaginary dais,
 He's piled high with many cushions.

He would prefer the Japanese,
Whose hair spread out upon her pillow,
Sleeps like a black cat,
Purring in his ear.

You see,
He dreams,
Though he does not wait,
But sleeps in the louche district of red lights,
Dreaming of the waiting woman left behind,
Who waits, and dreams, and works,
And combs her jet black hair before a mirror,
Reflecting only her.

He waits behind the mirror,
Watching, waiting,
Musing the obscure,
Not giving what is real,
That's more perfect and serene,
Through what any other motion,
Causing action might restore.

Related to Sacred Places
We have Traveled

She was called to visit,
Sacred places:
The ruins of temples,
Venerable shrines,
And the altars of sacrifice.

She heard their spirits,
Whisper to her,
In bedtime stories,
While she slept,
And sing soft lullabies,
While she rested,
Urging her,
To pause fast-forward's,
Numbing pace,
And claim tomorrow's fate.

Not always welcome,
Is the silence,
Of a quiet mind,
Not inhabited ,
By a feckless,
Dull routine,

For in the quiet,
Can be heard,
The doleful refrain,
Of the traveling minstrel's,
Tune.

She answered to a call,
So inexact,
It may as well,
Have been,
A foreign stranger,
Dialing the wrong number,
In the middle,
Of the night.

It was enough,
To wake her up,
And heed the urge,
To travel,
To far-off,
Sacred places.
Knowing…
To refuse,
Was not an option.

Directions to our destinations,
Are seldom ever written,
More often spoken,
In the glossoalia of dead languages,
Broadcast from the catwalks of minarets,
Or sung by choirs,
In the houses of worship,
Or in the drone of prayers,
Chanted by five- thousand devotees,
Gathered In,
Saint Mark's Square.

You shall meet,
The spirit said,
At the Temple of Artemis,
Whose goddess,
It commemorates,
In everlasting stone,
Is imprisoned in a foreign land,
Confined to history's prison.
Much like your shared life has become,
To each a cold and distant companion.

Lost…they said,
But remembered,
Is your history.
Needing a revision,
Or altogether forgotten,
And put aside.
Your obligation,
Daunting,
For you must…
Compose,
A new edition.

He is…
Like a Pilgrim,
Cowed before the guru,
Seeking blessings at his feet,
He paid the vigorish of salvation,
And began his penance there.

He was granted partial absolution,
Much added cost applied,
Not entirely forgiven,
But his dignity restored,
And all scapegrace left behind.

You were told,
To climb the slopes,
Of Ayasoluk Hill,
By each a separate path,
And visit the city,
Of Ephesus,
Restored, ironically,
As ruins,
And, in reaching it,
Continue climbing on,
Although the grade's no longer steep,
And discover in this philosophic,
Simple riddle,
A new direction,
And a better purpose,
To your lives.

Your existential questions,
Were answered,
In childish riddles,
By addled prophets,
Dressed as beggars,
Selling talismans,
To desperate seekers,
While stealing shekels,
From their purses.

You heard promises of cures,
For loneliness,
And all of life's
Infirmities, scourges,
And addictions,
There were herbs for sale,
That would make you,
Strong,
And also a better lover,
There were the glassy lunes,
Of the evil eye,
To deflect,
The curses of your enemies.

He bought the charm,
That guaranteed an end,
To his pursuit of isolation,
That would unite him,
With another,
Who sought to do the same.

It was a false, cheap,
Chinese trinket,
That he bought...
So, he tossed it in a well.

There is no substitute,
The spirit said,
For hard work,
In earning what is precious,
Something that will outlast,
A nation,
Even though what,
You make that's new,
Is built upon a ruin.

There is beauty,
In the synthesis of parts,
And broken things.
A speculated whole,
Assembled from 10,000,
Puzzle pieces,
Now much stronger,
And closer to perfection,
Than before.

He gives you,
A precious relic,
That is real.

Possessed of,
Genuine spirit,
And infused with forces,
Which bind the heavens,
And the earth.
And therefore,
You and him.

He pried it from the foundation,
Of the holiest church,
Of classical time,
When the land was ruled,
By powerful gods,
And all mankind,
Believed in miracles,
And there were saints,
Who walked among us,
Who were not all madmen,
Burning with the fever,
Of crimson visions,
But spoke to us,
Of hope.

The Basilica of St. John,
The Apostle,
Is from where this relic came.

Created, it is said,
In the womb,
Of the universe,
And placed in the Apostle's hand.
A rare, stony-iron artifact,
Made of elements unknown,
Fashioned in a manner,
Beyond the unaided,
Power of man…
And it bears the prophet's brand.

This isn't an Aesop's fable,
Or a fiction,
Based in scripture.
Truth is in the story,
Of the "Theologian" saint.

The story's told,
That St. John's body sleeps,
Beneath twins pillars,
Of the ruin,
And that when he breathes,
This dust appears,
In a ring,
Around his tomb.

Those who make the journey,
May take the manna home.
They are granted,
Grace, and healing,
And the apostle's
Absolution.

Though the Guardians,
 Of the Mysteries,
Say the manna is a gift,
From god,
It is not,
Freely given.
 It's only gotten,
When the price,
Is paid.

We are commanded to continue,
Performing self-less acts,
Of kindness,
And in a life lived,
Fully and with purpose,
Our holiness arrives,
On the blessings,
They bestow.

I encourage you,
To take heart,
And trust the grace,
He's earned.

For, in the dust,
The scree,
And scattered rocks,
Of ruins,
There is hope,
And no need,
For either of you,
To be alone.

Speak False, Love True

In the years I have held forth,
My love and my devotion,
Offering puerile verses,
And love sonnets,
In a vacillating voice,
Alternately faltering and clear,
Laced with sighs and hesitations,
Inept and clumsy,
In my execution.

My declarations of love,
Were slips- of- the- tongue,
Near misses and approximations,
Of what I felt.
And how did I score with her?
Always a failure,
Because I sounded insincere.

She said I played false,
When I spoke true,
At least in my estimation I did,
Because of numerous near misses,
And with most successes,
Partly failures,
Whenever I would try,
To put the right words,
 Into her vernacular.

I once wrote the words down,
To get beyond the fundamentals,
Of a simple, "I love you,"
Because to her,
Such economy of words,
Is woefully bereft,
Of her expectation,
For elaboration.

And so I memorized,
What I had written down,
And improvised before the mirror,
Before delivering my soliloquy,
To her.

Ugh…she booed me from the stage,
Like a royal patron,
Throwing rotted fruit,
And insults,
At a bad Shakespearean actor.

She said I had the diction of a yokel,
And the coaching of a hack,
And that all my lines,
Communicated a shallow plot,
To get her in the sack.

I tried to articulate the truth,
Of my deep love,
In pure, unmediated ways,
From dialogue that - okay - began,
With trying to make perfectly good sense,
But my good intentions,
Invariably…
Ended in collapse.

She finally put it straight to me,
That my efforts were a waste,
That a man who cannot declare his love,
With romance, dance and passion,
Is a sorcerer without magic,
A prophet without god.

My solution to the problem,
Was quite simple,
I should have figured it out sooner:
Don't be slippery, verbose or glib,
Don't act the galliard,
Don't get down on bended knee.
You may quote French and Italian phrases,
And a 'roses- are- red' poem or two.

So, be an empty container,
Into which her words,
Of self-love will fill.
An echo chamber,
Out of which she'll hear,
What she desires,
As though coming from you.

May I leave it to such wisdom:
That to make my words of love,
Sound true,
Be intentionally vague,
Even quiet and intentionally obscure.

Let her fill your empty word container,
With the echoes of her thoughts,
Which she'll understand,
Much better than your words.

For in your silence,
And your pie-eyed adoration,
You are wise…
Even profound.

She'll have all the love she needs,
Because it's coming all from her,
And coming from the source,
It has no pretense, insincerity,
Or bounds.

Judas Kiss

You were there,
Like the green flash,
Of the nautical dawn,
Ephemeral, transitory and rare,
A singularity and accidental gift,
To the weary and habitual traveler,
Most difficult to inspire,
But for you.

I did not expect to see you here,
Amidst a sea of unfamiliar faces,
All strangers speaking foreign languages,
And everyone in a hurry.

How unexpected is that,
To meet again by chance,
Or was it fate,
In which I don't believe,
Perhaps then a rare coincidence,
Or just plain happenstance.

A match struck in a cave
Will flare bright and blind,
Organic moving things,
Accustomed to an indelible world,
And whose numbed extremities,
Cannot read the map,
Etched along,
The cold, sharp craggy wall,
Within the beguiler's,
Secret cave.

You appeared just as Genesis mentioned light,
And changed a preternatural shadow world,
Through which I blindly groped,
When rose an orb of fire,
Like a golden monstrance
Announcing creation's first horizon.

I am too lofty with description,
Trying to charm you like the fakir,
Who plays the shrill punji,
To wake the sleeping cobra,
Causing it to dance and swoon,
In time,
With his seductive tune.

Perhaps it was…
Just a busy public place,
Lit up with garish electric lights,
I mistook for an avenue more sublimed,
Like Heinlein's galactic cities,
Not Las Vegas Strip,
Whose neon is all buzz and sizzle,
Flickering and shorting in a summer drizzle,
Where sex sets fire to the rain,
And where it's never dark,
And no one ever sleeps,
And all the damned pay visit.

Still and all it is amazing,
Seeing you here.
I should have never doubted,
I would spot you,
In the crowd,
If only to intercept your path,
Precisely paved,
In opposite directions.

You did not wear the crown I made,
And placed upon strawberry scented hair,
For it was perishable,
And would only last one season.
A wreath,
Made out of ivy spliced with baby's breath,
And bejeweled with Jerusalem cherries.

Your samite blouse,
Is now a chambray frock,
Though still your carmine lips,
Might rouse and tempt me,
If I obsess or linger,
Any longer here.

A tentative hug,
And then a kiss for old time's sake,
That set no fire to the memories,
That would remain unspoken,
And give up no tears,
Or spontaneous love verses,
No terms of endearment,
No laments of piteous remorse,
For that enchanted summer.

Dry has become the riverbed,
Of our past sailing days,
All white chalk and cracked salt flats,
Like parched Nevada,
And the Dead Sea shores of Galilee.

I did not turn around,
And watch you walk away,
I didn't want to see the sun dip down,
Or witness the waxing,
Of the full pearlescent moon.

In memory and in me,
There is a soft eternal flame,
Lit long ago by you,
That will last,
Like the chatoyant glimmer,
Of a precious gem,
And the gleam of a cat's eye stone.

Whatsoever, things were just,
And pure,
And there was virtue,
Once upon a time…
So give thanks,
And praise sincere.

Though you be guided,
To your final destination,
With Astarte and Anath at each sleeve,
And the lilies and the serpents at your feet,
With twisted briars for a crown,
I travel east and you go west,
And each of us,
Will climb a hill,
And sit alone,
In silent,
Empty,
Contemplation,
There.

Haiku…Yuck!

Feather floating down
Riding a soft summer breeze
Bird killed by a hawk

Black kid on the block
What's his name and who cares?
Shot in a drive by

Snow bends a young oak
A burden not uncommon
An ice storm breaks it

Haiku

Too brief, too Asian
Sufficient for short people
Just into small talk

www.ingramcontent.com/pod-product-compliance
Lightning Source LLC
Chambersburg PA
CBHW032019040426
42448CB00006B/669